Where Did All the Water Go?

by Carolyn Stearns
illustrated by David Aiken

For Emily & Colleen
David Aiken

Tidewater Publishers
Centreville, Maryland

7 1 19

I wake up every morning, and what do I see? I see water, lots and lots of water. I live with my mom and dad in a house on Herring Bay, which faces the Chesapeake Bay. I usually see the sun, too, a big ball of fire looking at me as I squint at it. Then there are the geese and swans, and all the ducks and gulls and other birds in the sky.

But on this cold morning I wake up and something is wrong—really wrong. At first I'm too sleepy to figure out what it is. But then I do.

The water is gone. I don't see the water anywhere.

I dress myself and run outside.

"Where did all the water go?" I yell to the sky.

The sky doesn't pay any attention to me. All I can see are the swans, flying about and looking around for the water just as I am. They're making funny little wonking sounds from the inside of their throats as they look left and right.

A great blue heron flies by. "Hey, Heron," I yell. "Where did all the water go?"

The heron makes a sound like a car horn as it glides past me. The heron is looking for the water, too.

The mallard ducks are all in a tizzy, and the gulls are screeching as they zip this way and that. The canvasbacks are gone. No one knows where the water is.

When my mom and dad come out to see what all the fuss is about, I ask, "Where did all the water go? I went to bed last night and the water was here. Now, all I see are old pilings, an old shoe, two rusty tin cans, and a lot of sand and mud."

The swans, ducks, and gulls become very quiet. They want to know where the water is, too.

"Oh, I see a little water left," says my dad, pointing toward the horizon.

"But that's not enough water to fill a bathtub! I want to know where all the water is now!"

"Actually, the wind pushed the water away," says my dad. "That happens in the winter around the time of a full moon, like now."

"But the water was here last night," I shout. My dad is looking very tall this morning.

"I know," he said, "but remember how hard the wind was blowing all day yesterday? Remember how the house shook last night?"

"Yes."

"Well, the wind was coming from the northwest, near where the sun sets, and it was blowing so hard that the

tide couldn't come in."

"The wind can't do that!" I say, all in a fluster.

"Yes, it can," says Mom. "The wind is so strong it can knock down trees, pick up boats—even blow down houses. I don't mean to frighten you, but the wind can do many things. We need to respect it."

I imagine the wind blowing all the water to the opposite side of the Bay.

"Oh, those poor people living over there! Is the water over their heads?"

"I am sure no one is under the water," Mom says. "Don't you worry. Now that the wind has stopped, the tide can come back in, so the water will be back. If not today, tomorrow or the next day. You'll see."

"Really?"

"Yes, really," says my dad, with a tone in his voice that tells me I'm asking too many questions. Again.

"Still," I mumble to myself, "the water must be *some*where."

"I think the water is floating up in the sky," says a swan who waddles past us. "Up above the clouds."

"I think the water is hidden in an underground cave," says a gull sitting sullenly on a piling, "where it's real quiet."

"I think the water is spiraling down into a deep hole never to be seen again," quacks a duck fearfully. This duck is better at worrying than I am.

"Enough thoughts about water. It's time to get ready for school," says Mom. "Who knows, maybe the water will be back when you get home from school this afternoon."

I go to school because I have to, not because I want to. I worry the whole time. I can't imagine a life next to the Bay without water. What are all the birds, the fish, and the oysters to do? Are they going to die?

When the school day is finally over, I get back on the school bus and head home. Even though I know my dad will have my favorite cookies waiting for me, I want to stay on the bus forever. I close my eyes because I'm afraid of what I might see when the bus stops at my driveway. I imagine a sandy shore filled with lots and lots of dead fish and dried-up swans and ducks—all my best friends.

As the school bus turns the corner to my house, I squeeze my eyes even tighter shut.

"You're home," calls the bus driver. "Wake up!"

I keep my eyes pressed together and stagger down the center aisle of the bus.

"Hurry up," my dad calls. "I have a surprise for you."

I open my eyes a tiny crack and jump down the big step of the school bus.

"Look," he cries.

I do as my dad says. He's pointing toward the Bay.

"It's back!" I yell. "The water is back!"

My heart about bursts with joy. The water *is* back, all sparkly, bright, and blue-green. The geese are flying, the ducks are swimming, the gulls are gliding, the swans are arguing, and the oysters are—well, the oysters are doing whatever oysters do. Nothing has changed. And I don't see a single dead thing anywhere.

"Wow!" I yell as I run to greet the water.

When I reach the water's edge, I stop short and whisper, "Welcome back, Water. I missed you!"

I can't say for sure the water heard me, but it did throw some spray up in my face at that very moment.

Where *Does* All the Water Go?

When a strong storm hits the Chesapeake Bay region in the wintertime, its northeast winds can push large amounts of water from the ocean up into the Bay. This causes very high tides.

If the moon is full after the storm passes, and cold, clear air from Canada brings northwest winds to the Bay, then much of the pent-up water is rapidly pushed back out to the ocean. Even after these winds die down, high pressure from the cold, dense air settling in pushes down on the surface of the Bay. This keeps the water level low—so low it disappears in the very shallow places, and many areas that are usually underwater can be seen.